George Herriman, in an undated photo (found as part of the Swinnerton estate and sent as a gift to Louise Swinnerton) c. late 1930s-early1940s. Courtesy Mr. Robert L. Beerbohm.

 KRAZY & IGNATZ.

by George Herriman.

"Love Letters in Ancient Brick."

Continuing the Complete Full-Page Comic Strips,

1927-28.

Edited by Bill Blackbeard.

Fantagraphics Books, SEATTLE.

KRAZY KAT By Her

Published by Fantagraphics Books.
7563 Lake City Way North East,
Seattle, Washington. 98115. United States of America.

Edited and annotated by Bill Blackbeard.
Except where specified, all research materials appear courtesy of the San Francisco Museum of Cartoon Art.
Designed and Decorated by Chris Ware.
Promoted by Eric Reynolds.
Published by Gary Groth and Kim Thompson.

First Fantagraphics Books edition: October 2002.

ISBN 1-56097-507-3.

Printed in Canada by WestCan Printing Group, Winnipeg, Manitoba.

Thanks to Robert L. Beerbohm,
Mary Ann Brandon, and
Charles Valauskas for their help
in assembling this volume.

man **KRAZY & IGNATZ.**

PILFERING MRS. KWAK-WAK'S GOOD OLD GOODS AND GOODIES BAG: SCOOP THE FIRST

Introduction by Bill Blackbeard.

IT MUST BE A NIGHTMARE OR SOMETHING

It is notorious in the ways and byways of the desert County yclept Coconino that the fussbudget and gossip known roundabout as Mrs Kwak-Wak has compiled dossiers of dirt on the doings of Allan Sundry and everyone else who walks in the shadow of the Old Smoke Tree. These choice bits of chatter and chit-chat, which range from the domestic drama of the Ignatz Mouse ménage, the dread nocturnal deliveries of Joe Stork, the choice membership in the club of Offisa Pupp, and the sweetly inventive katerwauls of the kat called Krazy, to the bizarre and epic career of the coy creator of the County itself, Gargeous George Herriman the human hatrack, whose intimately inimitable amblings of pen and fancy frolic unfettered through most of the fey pages of this tasty tome. Although Mrs K-W sows her accumulated arcana broadcast on any provocation, its repository is to be found in no actual grip, case, or bag limned by Herriman (not even in the dowager duck's ubiquitous umbrella) but solely in her capacious and crowded cabeza. Since the open probing and plundering of this trove could scarcely be undertaken without mortally offending the good lady, we have taken leave (no, not yet of our meager wits) to invent an external and parallel container, a handy symbolic cache of the delightful detritus squirreled away by this dear duck. And we have taken an initial sampling of this trove to spread before your ineffably dazzled eyes in the pages that turn here and ahead, a kind of prefatory anticipation of the following two years of the great Sunday page work that is central to this continuing retrieval of what Bill Fields might have termed George Herriman's opus giganticus, *Krazy Kat.*

A cherished tidbit of Kwak-Wakian scandal broke nationally on September 17, 1922, when self-styled expert desert trekkers George Herriman and Jimmy Swinnerton had to be saved from their own confused expedition into the Arizona desert in search of a bizarre "blue waterfall" by local Hopi Indians. The original Hearst news story, reprinted above, appeared in the *New York Sunday American.* Though Herriman later spent several years drawing a daily cartoon panel feature titled "Embarrassing Moments" for the Hearst comics syndicate, as far as is known, he did not limn his own performance in redface in the panel series: a pity, since it would certainly have given us an otherwise non-existent Herriman caricature of Swinnerton.

2 CARTOONISTS LOST IN DESERT MAZES

Creators of "Krazy Cat" and "Little Jimmy" Saved from Death by Arizona Indians.

George Herriman and James Swinnerton, the cartoonist creators of "Krazy Cat" and "Little Jimmy," almost perished two weeks ago when they lost their way in a regular labyrinth of steep cliffs in the heart of the Arizona desert.

The two artists for forty-eight hours tried vainly to find the narrow "hole in the way" by which they had entered. They had eaten the last of their food when two friendly Hopi Indians, seeing their horses browsing outside rescued them.

Swinnerton and Herriman had expected never to leave the place alive.

The two men, who are familiar with the Southwest country, set out to find a "blue waterfall" which Swinnerton desired to paint. Search for water led them to enter the narrow aperture, but no sooner had they done so than a dense fog hid the entrance from them. When the fog lifted, efforts to find it were futile, as all the cliffs looked just alike.

Embarrassing Moments

Embarrassing Moments

Embarrassing Moments

Embarrassing Moments

Embarrassing Moments

Embarrassing Moments

George Herriman and Billy De Beck (of Barney Google and Snuffy Smith fame) drew the "Embarrassing Moments" panel gag series over a five year period in the 1920s for the Hearst Newspapers. One of the two cartoonists would draw the panels for upwards of a year or so, then the other would take on the job. Unsigned and without a printed byline, "Embarrassing Moments" was used by the Hearst papers as a space filler on their daily comic pages. (Sometimes De Beck would lodge tongue firmly in chic and sign his EM panels "Barney Google.") This selection is made up of Herriman panels that touch in part on his cartoonist life. (A full-size original "Embarrassing Moments" appears in the 1925-1926 volume.)

How Ignatz Mouse's Perseverance Overcame Krazy Kat's Good Luck--By Herriman

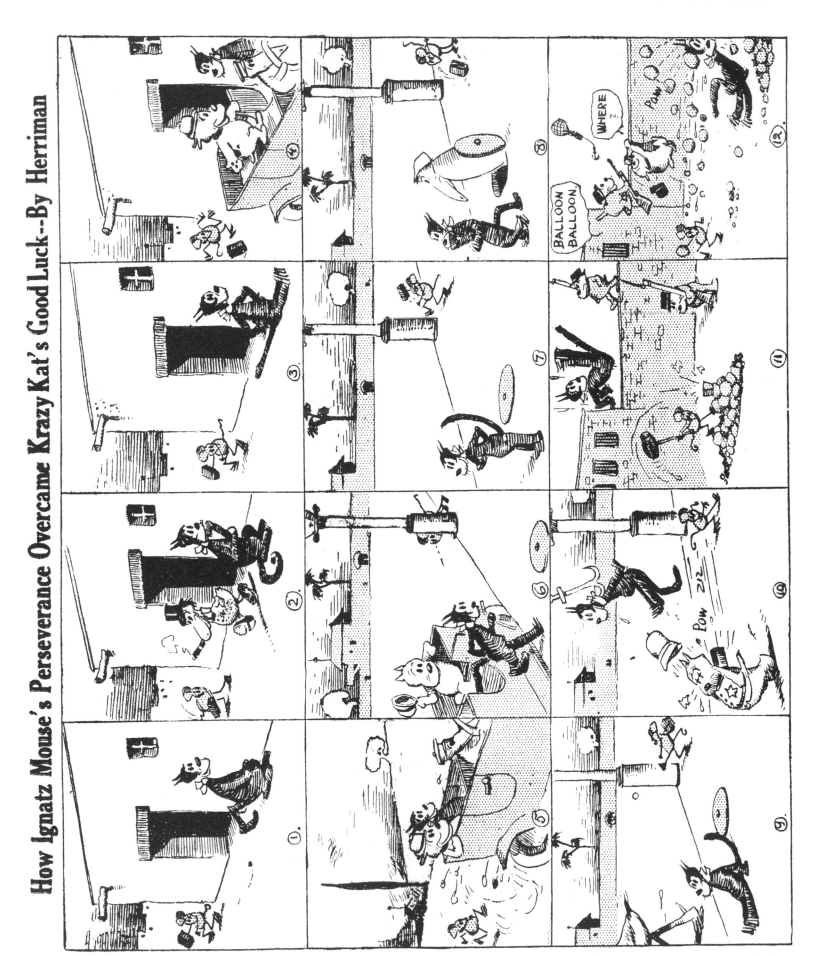

Remember---A Swinnerton Joke Book Next Sunday!

A choice treasure from the Kwak-Wak lode is this 1914 full-page forerunner of the Krazy Kat Sunday page series, which began in 1916. It appeared in a one-shot Hearst Sunday paper tabloid section titled "The Dingbat Family's Joke Book" by George Herriman. The black and white tab section, made up of some Herriman cartoon work plus many printed jokes and gag art from minor cartoonists, was one of a series of "Joke Book" sections, each based on the work of a comic artist working in the Hearst bullpen of the time, including Swinnerton, Nell Brinkley, Tad Dorgan, H. H. Knerr, etc. The cover of the Herriman Joke Book appears on the following page.

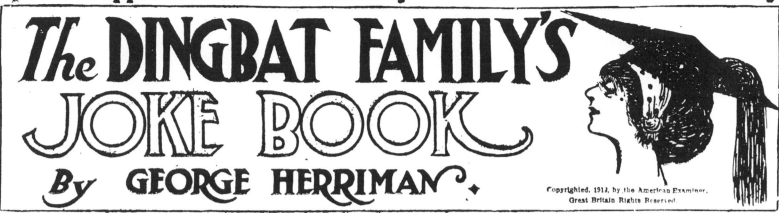

The DINGBAT FAMILY'S JOKE BOOK
By GEORGE HERRIMAN

Little Mr. Dingbat's Burden---By Herriman

Krazy Kat Herriman
Loves His Kittens — **By T. E. Powers**
Copyright, 1922, by Star Company.

KEEPING UP WITH THE JONESES—Yes, Pa Can Tell. —By POP.

CAT TALES. —By POP.

CAT TALES —By POP

In this national political page cartoon for the Hearst papers of 7/25/22, Herriman's old bullpen buddy from the 1910s in New York, T. E. Powers, speculates amusingly on the (unlikely) origin of THE kat. Notorious as Hearst's favorite political cartoonist, Powers worked for the Hearst chain from the 1910s into the 1950s. To eyes other than Hearst's, Powers' graphic work seemed weak-minded and unimaginative, and the idea that Hearst could prefer Powers to the powerful Winsor McCay, who also put in many years on the Hearst editorial pages, was all but inconceivable to most cartoonists. This unusual example of Powers' craft in a sentimentally humorous vein, however, seems worth preserving among Mrs Kwak-Wak's omnivorous gatherings.

Herriman's highly innovative notion of pursuing a separate comic strip conflict under the feet of his principal strip characters in The Dingbat Family (a Hearst daily strip in the 1910s) delighted the public and "inspired" a number of sometimes lesser cartoonists to imitate the idea. Mrs. K-W ferreted one 1914 example from the work of Price Allman, whose *Doings of the Duffs* was a considerable national success until the artist sent a month's worth of strip episodes to his syndicate in which the Duffs appeared minus noses ("I just got tired of drawing noses," he said); Arthur R "Pop" Momand, whose *Keeping Up With the Joneses* ran for decades in dozens of paper, was the source of these two remaining clips. Doubtless, many newspaper readers credited Allman and Momand with this seemingly novel idea of a double strip, since the Hearst papers which almost exclusively ran the Herriman Dingbat strip appeared in only a handful of large cities on the perimeter of the nation. Even Cliff Sterrett, one of the greatest cartoonists of the period, adopted the Herriman idea for a few weeks, but did so as bullpen gag to entertain Herriman. Sterrett's underfoot concept was somewhat more integrated with the adult strip characters in his Polly and Her Pals than Herriman's, since his was a crawling baby.

A Canadian cartoonist named Arch Dale came up with the only successful full scale *Krazy Kat* imitation ever published, complete with an officious cop. Little seen in the states, Dale's *The Doodads* was widely printed in Canada in the 1920s with accompanying reprint albums, toys, and the like. The page appears to have been printed only in tabloid format, usually in full color; and there was also a daily. The strip did not survive the 1930s, although it was obviously an entertaining work while it lasted.

THE AMOURS OF MARIE ANNE MAGEE

THE PROFESSOR (10000 A. D.)—These, my child, are the remains of an extinct animal called the automobile. It was used as beast of burden in about the twentieth century, many thousand years ago.

THE DIFFERENCE

Leave it to the gossip biddy of Coconino County to find and sock away these bizarre remnants of the fledgling career of a great cartoonist. In the episode from "The Amours of Marie Anne McGee," a self-peddled daily strip sold as a package of twenty episodes, we find the raucous slapstick elements characteristic of Herriman's Sunday page work of the 1901-09 period. (This episode appeared in a small-town paper on 8/31/09, which is when the editor chose to run it; there was, of course, no syndicate release date.)

"Ah, but Miss Cashleigh, I have got zee title, and in Europe it tells you who is who."
"Yes, Count, and I have the money, which in America tells you what's what."

CONSOLING THOUGHT

"Chee, Willie, if it wuzn't fer us dem funny fellers'd starve."

"Don't be so pessimistic, Weary. Tink of all de free advertisement we gits."

The other five cartoons on these two pages appeared on April 5 and 6 on the editorial page of the Hearst *San Francisco Examiner,* together with gag cartoons from other hands, obviously reprinted from the Hearst Los Angeles Examier, where Herriman was employed as general graphic humor factotum at the time, drawing his early *Baron Mooch* daily comic strip, sports page cartoons, and editorial cartoons as needed. The amount of high fancy in several of these cartoons is remarkable for the period.

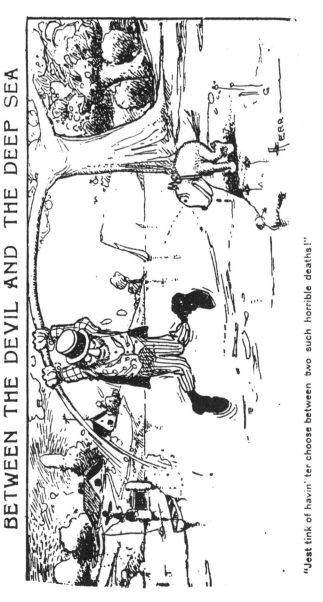

BETWEEN THE DEVIL AND THE DEEP SEA

"Jest tink of havin' ter choose between two such horrible deaths!"

THE OLD SONG IN FUTURE DAYS

If a lassie meets a laddie coming thro' the clouds, etc.

(Copyright, 1920, by The Lewis Publishing Co.)

GEORGE HERRIMAN—PROGENITOR OF KRAZY KAT AND THE IRASCIBLE IGNATZ, THE BRICK-HEAVING MOUSE

Being Some Inside Information as Furnished by the
Authorities and the Wife
of the Accused.

Written Expressly for the
Sunday Magazine

By ROY L. McCARDELL

Pictures by Herriman and Bob Dean

He Would Come to Serenade His Love on
Moonlight Nights.

George Herriman and the Wife He Loves
Best of All.

Drawn for the Occasion by George Herriman.

SOME twenty-two years ago there was in Los Angeles, Cal., a one-cylinder barber shop of great age, and around this barber shop there was a young shaver, too, of, the proprietor, by the name of George Herriman.

This was in the days before the marvelous motion-pictures attracted so many people to the City of Angels, and ere the population surpassed that of San Francisco.

Los Angeles in those times was a dusty, straggling town, frequented by cowboys, Mexicans, fruit growers, not many tourists and no picture stars, picture supes, picture directors who only think in millions.

In those days there were no flivvers or cafeterias in that part of California, and the cowboys hitched their horses to giant cactuses and tourists kodaked the horses so hitched and sent the snapshots back home marked: "The Cucumbers Grow So Big Out Here That They Hitch Horses to Them."

YOUNG HERRIMAN had all the proper qualifications of a barber—except loquacity. He could play the guitar and sing "The Spanish Cavalier," "Two Little Girls in Blue" and "My Old New Hampshire Home." He sang the last with great pathos and feeling, because the only old New Hampshire home he had ever known was Los Angeles.

Then oe eventful night he told his beloved that always wearing this.

THEY oe eventful night he told his beloved that two great opportunities it life had opened up for him.

One was a job at a dairy on the outskirts of Los Angeles in which his duties were to consist of leading real estate boomers on the plates, and going out and bringing in a van of beer ever and anon to lay the dust.

He soon decided—our hero did—that he could draw pictures himself—although Andy Barber would never permit him—telling him to draw beer. So to prove he was an artist he drew a gigantic deep etching of a skull and cross bones on the first cement sidewalk ever received and declaimed that verse libre epic that all out...

HIS work improved and he got several raises of salary, which so encouraged him that he resolved that while Westward the Course of Empire might take its way; he was going to beat it for the East.

And beat it he did—he beat it in box cars, coal cars, gondolas, flats, blind baggage and every other way except on the cushions, leaving his fair young bride behind where she could get her meals regularly in papa's house and sit off the porch at eve and wonder if George was dead, as he hadn't written home for money for two weeks.

Arriving in New York, young Herriman found the art editors of the great metropolitan dailies singularly cold to his advance. They rejected the specimens of his art that he displayed as being too bizarre. He drifted to Coney Island and eked out a precarious livelihood, painting targets in shooting galleries.

In Coney Island, however, his art finally stood him in good stead, for learning that hot-dog mustard was made mainly of vegetable substances that cost at least ten cents a pound, ...

HE was next employed as an outdoor orator by Harry Tudor, who had the Bosco, the Snake Eater, concession at Coney Island at Dreamland, that season. It was while so employed that George Herriman first concocted ...

Roy L McCardell, poet, science fiction writer, Hollywood scripter, editor, was a one-man whirlwind of variant creative activity in the 1890s well into the next century. He wrote a classic, very touching poem, "The Organ Man," for *Puck* in 1894, turned out popular fiction filler for the early pulps, including a Sam Moscowitz pick for his *Science Fiction by Gaslight*, "The Hybrid Hyperborean Ant," buddied with cartoonists as a *Puck* editor and later as a Hearst editor (where he suggested the idea for a full color cartoon art section in the Hearst New York Journal in 1893, which came to historic fruition three years later), then took up scripting for the youthful movie industry, writing "A Fool There Was" for Theda Bara. Yet the referential record is vague about McCardell in general, lacking birth and death dates, and further information on his fiction, editing, and scripting. There is not a word about him, for example, in Moses Koenigsberg's *King News*, an anecdote- and personality-packed volume dealing at length with the Hearst comics empire and its cartoonists. *Google* renders naught, nor do the literary, theatrical, and film referentia of the past century. He did, however, write a memorable short work on comic strips of his time, " Opper, Outcault, and Company," for the old *Everybody's Magazine* of June, 1905 (reprinted in *Inks* for May of 1995), and the piece reprinted on these pages, as it first appeared in the Sunday edition of the New York theatrical newspaper, *The Morning Telegraph*, for August 22, 1920. (Possibly this late date for a McCardle byline suggests that he may have disappeared into the *Telegraph* editorial limbo in later years.) Mrs Kwack-Wak's scouring of the Coconino social and literary terrain has certainly yielded no long-buried treasure to surpass this.

1927.

KRAZY KAT   By Herriman

January 2nd, 1927.

KRAZY KAT   By Herriman

January 9th, 1927.

"G. NAUFEL AWFEL, D.D." (DOCTOR OF DESTINY) - MOLDER OF MEN, MICE AND MISCELLANY, KNEADS A BATCH OF PASTE IN THE SECRET LABORATORY ON THE "ENCHANTED MESA" - WHERE "JOE STORK" LIVES - PURVEYOR OF PROGENY TO PRINCE, & PROLETARIAT.

THIS LETS YOU IN ON A BIT OF CONVERSATION - WHICH SHOWS HOW MUCH, AND HOW LITTLE "PARENTS" HAVE TO DO WITH IT ———

Q. IN THE INTERIM LITTLE "EPPIS", AN ORPHAN "APPENDIX", HOMELESS, SIN MADRE, Y SIN PADRE, - THAT IS - SANS MÈRE, ET SANS PÈRE, COMES FROM WE KNOW NOT WHERE - TO FIND ITSELF ATOP THE "MESA ENCANTADA" - A SITUATION WHICH CAUSES IT TO ASPIRATE A WORD, OR TWO OF SINCERE WONDERMENT

HAVE "APPENDIXES" KURIOSITY? HAH - WE'LL SAY THEY HAVE - AT LEAST THIS ONE HAS.

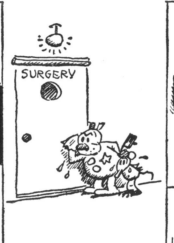

IT HAD TO HAVE, OR THERE WOULD HAVE BEEN NO EXCUSE FOR US TO WRITE THESE WITLESS WORDS, OR PEN THESE PUSILLANIMOUS PICTURES ———

A SPAN OF A CERTAIN AMOUNT OF YEARS, AND FROM KITTEN HOOD TO KATHOOD IT GREW, ASTUTE, ADROIT, AND AMIABLE - BEARING THE NAME "KRAZY" - ONE DAY CAME A PAIN - A POWERFUL PAIN !!!

HERRIMAN

January 16th, 1927.

KRAZY KAT   By Herriman

January 23rd, 1927.

January 30th, 1927.

February 13th, 1927.

KRAZY KAT   By Herriman

February 20th, 1927.

February 27th, 1927.

March 6th, 1927.

KRAZY KAT   By Herriman

March 13th, 1927.

KRAZY KAT   By Herriman

March 20th, 1927.

Krazy Kat · · · · By Herriman

March 27th, 1927.

27.

April 3rd, 1927.

Krazy Kat ▪ ▪ ▪ By Herriman

AN ARENACEOUS EMPIRE — "KAIBITO" — A GRANULATE WORLD AWASH - FROM HORIZON TO HORIZON — WHICH IS A HEAP OF TERRITORY —

DAG NEBBIT — "IGNATZ" SAID, MEET HIM HERE - IN "KAIBITO"

"KRAZY KAT" A PASSENGER, AFOOT IN THIS PULVERULENT DOMAIN —

STOP.

ZIP

OOY - FOR A MOMINT, OR MAYBE A MINNIT I WILL GIVE MYSELF A REST WHILE I WAIT —

WHO IN A MOMENT OF FATIGUE SURRENDERS TO SLUMBER - IN AN ARENOSE EMBRACE .

SHUX, AND WE HAD SUCH A NICE, WHITE SNOW BLANKET WOVEN TO SPREAD OVER "KAIBITO" TODAY —

DON'T WORRY, THE WINDS WE WILL WAFT OVER KAIBITO THIS DAY WILL COVER MORE THAN ALL THE FRAYED, & FADED QUILTS YOUR SILLY LOOMS HAVE FASHIONED

WHILE IN THE CANYON CLEFTS, THE SNOW SQUAWS OF "SHONTO" MATCH STICKS WITH THE WIND WITCHES OF "WINANNI" — TO SEE WHETHER IT WILL SNOW, OR BLOW - IN KAIBITO — — THE WINDS WIN —

KAT, OR NO KAT, I'VE PACKED THIS "BRICK" OVER THIS DARN SAND LONG ENOUGH - I'LL BE LUCKY IF I CAN CARRY MY SELF BACK TO HARD PAN AGAIN —

AND AFTER THE "BIG WIND" CAME "IGNATZ."

ENNA WHERE — ENNA PLACE — ENNA HOW — HE FINDS ME LI'L "AINJIL"

HERRIMAN

April 10th, 1927.

Krazy Kat · · · · By Herriman

April 17th, 1927.

KRAZY KAT - - By Herriman

April 24th, 1927.

May 1st, 1927.

May 8th, 1927.

May 15th, 1927.

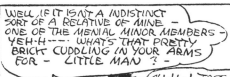

May 22nd, 1927.

May 29th, 1927.

KRAZY KAT - - By Herriman

June 6th, 1927.

KRAZY KAT - - By Herriman

June 13th, 1927.

KRAZY KAT ·· By Herriman

June 20th, 1927.

KRAZY KAT ·· By Herriman

KRAZY KAT, SUDDENLY AFFLICTED WITH AN ACUTE ADDICTION FOR SLUMBER, PROSTRATES HIMSELF BENEATH A NOBLE "ROBLE" - A "ROBLE" IF YOU MUST KNOW, IS AN "OAK".

WHILE NEAR BY, "IGNATZ" DOES THE SAME, HOWEVER, IN THE UMBRAGE OF AN "ALISO" -- AN "ALISO" IF YOU ASK, IS A "SYCAMORE" ——

"OFFICER PUPP" FEELING THE SAME URGE, SUCCUMBS IN THE SHADOWS OF A "FRESNO" - A "FRESNO" WE VENTURE TO SAY - IS AN "ASH"

A "STAR" WILL SHED ITS LIGHT, A "SNAKE" ITS SKIN - "CROCODILES" & "HUMANS", TEARS - AND "TREES" WILL SHED THEIR LEAVES —— OAK LEAVES BURY "KRAZY KAT", SYCAMORE LEAVES BLANKET "IGNATZ MOUSE", WHILE THOSE OF THE ASH HIDE "OFFICER PUPP" FROM VIEW

WELL

WELL -

WELL -

WELL, N'AFTER THAT, THE WIND WITCHES OF WINANI BREWED A BONNIE BREEZE - AND AS "LEAVES WILL", WHEN COMES A BREEZE - THEY LEAVE - BUT TWO REMAINED, WHO COO BEHIND A ROCK, T'WAS THEY WHO TOLD US THIS SILLY STORY - BUT WHO BELIEVES "LEAVES"?

HERRIMAN

June 27th, 1927.

July 4th, 1927.

KRAZY KAT · · By Herriman

July 11th, 1927.

KRAZY KAT - - By Herriman

July 18th, 1927.

July 25th, 1927.

KRAZY KAT ∴ By Herriman

August 1st, 1927.

KRAZY KAT ∴ By Herriman

August 8th, 1927.

46.

KRAZY KAT ⋅⁚⋅ By Herriman

August 15th, 1927.

KRAZY KAT ∙:∙ By Herriman

August 22nd, 1927.

48.

August 29th, 1927.

KRAZY KAT ∴ By Herriman

September 4th, 1927.

September 11th, 1927.

KRAZY KAT ∻ By Herriman

September 18th, 1927.

KRAZY KAT ∴ By Herriman

September 25th, 1927.

KRAZY KAT -:- By Herriman

October 2nd, 1927.

KRAZY KAT ⁘ By Herriman

October 9th, 1927.

KRAZY KAT ⋅∶⋅ By Herriman

A MALARIA GERM, ON HIS WAY TO NO PARTICULAR PLACE, NIPS "KRAZY KAT'S" TOE TIP, AND SAUNTERS ON

IN DUE TIME, A "CHILL" SHIVERS HIS SOUL —

NEXT IS THE VERY CORE OF HIS SPIRIT, SEARED, AND SCORCHED BY THE FERVID FLAMES OF A FEVER

SHUX — I CAN'T SOKK A "KAT" WITH A CHILL — I'LL GET HIM A HOT WATER BOTTLE.

NOW, HE'S STEAMING WITH A FEVER — I MUST ALSO GET HIM A CHUNK OF "ICE"

HERE YOU ARE — ONE OF THESE IS FOR YOUR "CHILL" AND THE OTHER IS FOR YOUR "FEVER".

ONE FOR MY "CHILL" AND ONE FOR MY "FEEVA", BUT WHICH IS FOR WHICH — I DUNT KNOW.

AH — HE SLUMBERS WITH GREAT PEACE — A SURE SIGN THAT THAT EVIL "MOUSE" HAS NOT PESTERED HIM TODAY —

HERRIMAN

October 16th, 1927.

KRAZY KAT ⋅:⋅ By Herriman

October 23rd, 1927.

KRAZY KAT ∻ By Herriman

October 30th, 1927.

KRAZY KAT :•: By Herriman

November 6th, 1927.

KRAZY KAT ⁛ By Herriman

November 13th, 1927.

November 27th, 1927.

December 18th, 1927.

KRAZY KAT :•: By Herriman

December 25th, 1927.

1928.

KRAZY KAT   By Herriman

January 1st, 1928.

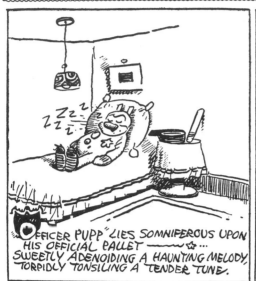

January 8th, 1928.

KRAZY KAT ❖ ❖ By Herriman

January 15th, 1928.

KRAZY KAT   By Herriman

January 22nd, 1928.

KRAZY KAT

By Herriman

January 29th, 1928.

KRAZY KAT

WHY SHOULD I GO TO A PLACE I'VE NEVER SEEN WHEN I'VE JUST BEEN THERE?

"BUM "BILL" BEE, RETURNING FROM WHENCE HE HAD NOT BEEN, PAUSES ON HIS WAY THERE, AND WITH HIS USUAL ENERGETIC INERTIA CHANGES HIS MIND —

HAH- AN INSTRUMENT OF TORTURE, FASHIONED BY WILLING HANDS TO SOOTHE AN ACHE.

HIS NEXT STEP A GREAT DISTANCE AWAY BY RAIL, AND LESS AFOOT BRINGS TO HIS VIEW, A "BRICK" - UPON WHICH HE LIGHTLY LAYS A HEAVY EYE IN UTTER DISREGARD -

I HAVE NO USE FOR A "BRICK" SO I'LL LOSE IT WHERE SOME ONE CAN HAVE A DIFFICULTY IN FINDING IT EASILY.

TURNING A CORNER IN A STRAIGHT LINE, HE VOICES A SILENT WORD, OR TWO, WHICH MEANS A VAST DEAL OF NOTHING —

GIVE ME - GIVE ME - GIVE ME -

SURE, IF YOU DON'T WANT IT, TAKE IT -

IT IS SELDOM THAT HE SO OFTEN SHOWS SUCH SELFISH GENEROSITY, AND YET RETAINS THAT WHICH HE GIVES

OOY, A HOLE, I MUST LOOK THROUGH IT.

THERE IS A CERTAIN WISDOM ABOUT "MICE" THAT RENDERS THEM QUITE STUPID.

PHUUU -

RESUMING HIS JOURNEY, HE PERSISTENTLY RESISTS ANY DESIRE TO GO ANY PLACE BUT WHERE HE DISLIKES TO BE - AND VICE-VERSA -

"IGNATZ", WHERE ART HE?

IN ORDER NOT TO ANSWER YOUR AMPLE QUESTION I'LL WHISPER LOUDLY - -YONDER -

LIKE THE RIGHT TIME, HE IS OFTEN INCORRECT, AND SO DISPENSES MUCH OF A SMALL AMOUNT OF MISINFORMATION —

ARE THEY TOGETHER? IF SO - WHERE?

BOTH OF THEM ARE BOTH THERE, AND WITH THEM BOTH IS A "BRICK" - IF YOU MEAN WHAT I KNOW -

THERE ARE NO HALF WAY POINTS WITH HIM, HE IS ALWAYS AT BOTH ENDS NEAREST THE MIDDLE, THUS MAKING HIMSELF UNREASONABLY DISPENSIBLE

FATE !! YES SIR, FATE !!!

JAIL

AH-H-H - YES.

HERRIMAN

February 5th, 1928.

KRAZY KAT   By Herriman

February 12th, 1928.

KRAZY KAT ⟶ By Herriman

February 19th, 1928.

KRAZY KAT ∴ By Herriman

February 26th, 1928.

KRAZY KAT ·:· By Herriman

March 4th, 1928.

KRAZY KAT

By Herriman

March 11th, 1928.

March 18th, 1928.

KRAZY KAT   By Herriman

March 25th, 1928.

KRAZY KAT

April 1st, 1928.

KRAZY KAT

By Herriman

April 8th, 1928.

April 15th, 1928.

I̱T GREW WITH NO GREAT GUSTO — FRAIL, AND FRAGILE OF FRAME — SUPPLIANT AND SERVILE OF SPINE — A "MAPLE", SO FULL OF A PRETTY PROMISE OF POSSIBILITIES WHICH ITS INFIRMITY FORBIDS —

IT NEEDS A "TONIC" — YES SIR — I'D SAY IT NEEDED A MIGHTY STIFF, POWERFUL "TONIC" —

ṮHAT MAN OF MEDICINE, DR. VIAGGS TAYLOR, LAYS AN EARNEST STETHOSCOPIC EAR TO ITS HEART, AND FINDS IT WEAKLY ATHROB, SUSTAINING WITH A THIN WHITE LINE OF SAP, A MOIETY OF LIFE —

THIS "MAPLE" OFFERS NO GREAT AMOUNT OF SHADE — YET THERE BEING NO OTHER TREE ABOUT TO RENDER ME AN UMBRAGE — I MUST NEEDS SIP MY "TONIC" HERE —

OH LOOK — "LAW" IS ABOUT TO BE BROKEN —

FOR MAPIL SIRRIP IT SURE LOOKS LIKE WATER.

BUT, "OFFICER PUPP" WOULD YOU HAVE ME WASTE THIS "TONIC" — THIS WONDERFUL "TONIC"?

"TONIC" ME EYE OUT WITH IT — EVERY DROP OF IT — SAVVY — EVERY DROP

H — AH-H-H — ORDER —

JAIL.

"KRAZY" IS SURE A SMART BUSINESS PERSON — NEVER HAVE I SEEN SO SWIFT A SALE OF "MAPLE SAP" BEFORE

W̱ELL, IN TIME IT WAXED ROBUST — THIS "MAPLE" — IT GREW A GREAT GIANT — AND GAVE MUCH "SAP" — "SAP" FULL OF SOMETHING — AH-H-YES, FULL OF WHAT YOU CALL — "PEP" — "ZIP" — Y'KNOW —

April 22nd, 1928.

April 29th, 1928.

KRAZY KAT   By Herriman

May 6th, 1928.

KRAZY KAT

By Herriman

May 13th, 1928.

KRAZY KAT

By Herriman

May 20th, 1928.

KRAZY KAT   By Herriman

May 27th, 1928.

KRAZY KAT   By Herriman

June 3rd, 1928.

June 10th, 1928.

June 17th, 1928.

July 1st, 1928.

July 8th, 1928.

KRAZY KAT   By Herriman

July 15th, 1928.

July 22nd, 1928.

July 29th, 1928.

August 5th, 1928.

KRAZY KAT

By Herriman

August 19th, 1928.

KRAZY KAT by Herriman

August 26th, 1928.

Krazy Kat

September 2nd, 1928.

September 9th, 1928.

KRAZY KAT *by Herriman*

WHAT DO YOU MEAN, YOU'RE LOOKING FOR A QUIET PLACE TO SLEEP IN? — WHAT DISTURBED YOUR SLUMBERS LAST NIGHT?

OOY, DAHLIN'K !!!! WOTTA NIGHT — WOTTA NIGHT — THE NEXT DESERT I TRY TO SLEEP ON, YOU'LL HAVE TO PROVE TO ME, THAT IT'S SOUND-PROOF — OOY-YOOY-YOOY

AND, AS "KRAZY" TOLD IT TO "IGNATZ" "IGNATZ" TOLD IT TO US — BELIEVE IT, OR NOT ✳

YEE-OW YEE-OW WOW YOW-OW OW 9 10W

BR-ROOOM ZOOOOMMMW ROOM

IT WAS "WILD-KET" PEAK WOT COMMENCED IT, WEN THE THUNDA-NIDDILS BEGUN TO BOOM AND ROAR — SO I TOOK MY TARP, & MOVED.

I HAD A IDA THAT THE NEXT PLACE I PICKED WOULD BE CALM WITH PEACE BUT NO — THEM "ELLAPHINTS LEGS" GOT TO DENCING FOXES TROTS PLAYED BY "ORGAN ROCK" — OY.

CHU-CHUU- HUH CHUH TOOTOOOOT TOOTOOOOOT

HOW DID I KNOW I'D MOVED OVA BY "TRAIN ROCK" WOT DID EVERYTHING BUT LEAVE THE DEEPO? IYE-YIYE-YIYE

GZAN' DLANG GALANG GI GLANG GANG ZLANG GLUNG GLONG

MEGINE MY IMBERRASSMINT WHEN I FOUND MYSELF CLOSE UP BY "CHURCH ROCK" — AH-H-ME ---

KLAP KLAP KLAP KLAP KLAP KLAP KLAP

HERE IN MONUMINT WALLEY I THOUGHT I'D FIND SWEET SILINCE IN WHICH TO SLUMBA — BUT WHY SHOULD THEM SILLY "MITTINS" BREAK OUT WITH APPLAUSE — I DUNT KNOW —

YEE-OW YEE-OW OW BOOM-MMM ZOOM OW OW CHUU CHUU TOOTTOOT TOOOOOO GLANG DANG DONG KLAP KLAP KLAP

AAH-HAA-AA I DUNT WUNT TO SLEEP ANY WAY — THE GAP

AND WEN THEM "ECHO KLIFFS" REPEATED EVER'THING THEY HAD HEARD — WAM — I TOSSED UP A SPONGE & QUIT !!"

WHAT HO, OFFICER PUPP MAKE READY THE "JAIL" !!!

COMING

9-16

HERRIMAN

September 16th, 1928.

WORDS BY "US"

WATCHFULLY 'WAITING FOR CRIME, AND DISORDER TO CROSS HIS "BEAT" — "OFFICER PUPP" SURRENDERS TO "SLUMBER", AND SLEEPS OR AS THE BARDS WOULD LILT, & LAY IT, A "NAP AT NOON".

SAID BY PARTY WITH BLUE SPECS.

HOW DARE HE LET FALL UPON HIS EYES THE FULL FELL FLARE & GLARE OF THE COCONINO SUN? — EYES NOT HIS, BUT THE PEOPLES — EYES TO BE KEPT KEEN WITH SIGHT THAT NO SIN, OR EVIL CAN ELUDE THEM —

BY SAME PARTY.

WHAT NEED HAVE I FOR "BLUE GLASSES" — WHEN THE LAW OF THE LAND LIES HERE IN WANT OF THEM? — AM I THEN SO LOW AS NOT TO SPARE THEM TO THE BETTER CAUSE? — NAY, NOT I — NEIGH NEE.

A MOT, OR TWO FROM OFFICER PUPP.

GOSH !!! I'VE BEEN ASLEEP — YES, SIR — I JUST KNOW I'VE BEEN ASLEEP

A FOUR LETTA WOID, A HARD, SQUARE CUBE OF BAKED CLAY —

TOLD BY "OFFICER PUPP" IN PROSE, AND SURPRISE.

WELL, OF ALL THINGS, A "BLUE KAT" — I'VE SEEN 'EM BLACK, WHITE, YELLOW, BROWN, GRAY — BUT NEVER BLUE BEFORE.

"OFFICER PUPP" WAGS ON

AND NOW, A BLUE MOUSE WITH A BLUE BRICK" — BLESS MY BLUE EYE, NEVER HAVE I SEEN SO AZURE AN OUTFIT.

OFFICER PUPP STILL ENGAGES IN VERBIAGE.

"HOOPEE" WOULD YOU LOOK AT THAT BLUE MOUSE SOKK THAT "BLUE KAT" WITH A "BLUE BRICK" — JUST WHAT IGNATZ WOULD HAVE DONE TO "KRAZY KAT" — THAT IS, IF I'D LET HIM, THE WRETCH — WHICH I NEVER WILL —

ONLY A MEANINGLESS "SIGH", SO WE'LL LET OFFICER PUPP SAY IT HIMSELF.

OH-HMMMM —

PERSON WHO GAVE "OFFICER PUPP" THE "BLUE SPECS" — RETURNS, SAYING.

THE SUN HAS SET, AND LOST ITS STING HIS EYES NO LONGER NEED THE PROTECTIVE HUE OF MY BLUE GLASSES — I WILL RECLAIM THEM — DUTY HAS BEEN NOBLY DONE.

September 23rd, 1928.

September 30th, 1928.

October 7th, 1928.

KRAZY KAT *by Herriman*

October 14th, 1928.

October 21st, 1928.

© 1928. by Int'l Feature Service, Inc. Great Britain rights reserved. 11-4

November 4th, 1928.

107.

KRAZY KAT by Herriman

November 11th, 1928.

KRAZY KAT *by Herriman*

DON KIYOTI CHAIRMAN OF THE CENTRAL COMMITTEE - PRESENTS THE HON. MR WOUGH WUPH WUFF - MAYOR IN PROSPECT TO AN ASSEMBLAGE OF COCONINO'S BEST CITIZENS - IGNATZ MOUSE - OFFICER PUPP KOLIN KELLY, BRICK MERCHANT - AND KRAZY KAT - WHO GIVE HIM EYE - LEND EAR - AND PAY HOMAGE IN AUSPICIOUS ACCLAIM ~~~ HIP-HIP ~~~ **HOO-RAY !!!** ~~~

AS I GAZE WITH MY PROUD EYE INTO THE GLEAMING BEAM OF YOUR INTELLIGENT CONTOURS - I FEEL MYSELF INFLATED WITH THAT URGE - THAT SURGE OF VOTES WHICH WILL SEND ME WHOOPEE TO THAT POST OF HONOR - THAT PEDESTAL OF POWER - THAT SEAT OF SANCTITY - THE "MAYOR'S CHAIR" -

AND IT IS WITH THAT GESTURE OF VERITY AND PROBITY - SO INHERENT TO WE WUFFS - THAT I NOW PAUSE TO PROMISE - ~~~ THRICE WILL I REPAY - YEA - THRICE THREE FOLD WILL I GIVE BACK - THRICE THRICE WILL I RETURN THE HONOR - ESTEEM - AND HONOR YOU HAVE HEAPED UPON ME - BY MAKING ME YOUR "MAYOR"

I WILL ROUT OUT **VICE** - STALK, ROOT, AND BRANCH - THE "EVIL" OF "BRICK" TOSSING I WILL BANISH FROM OUR FAIR CITY - HIM WILL I SCOURGE - HIM WILL I FLAY, WITH THE FLAIL OF JUSTICE WHO SO MUCH AS CASTS A EYE UPON A "BRICK" -

VICE, ONCE ERADICATED FROM OUR MIDST, WILL LEAVE US WITH NO USE FOR "JAILS" - NO USE FOR "COPS" - THUS WILL OUR SWEET SOIL HAVE BEEN PURGED OF A DIRE DRAG UPON OUR PUBLIC WEALTH.

NOR WILL MY TRAVAIL STOP AT THE END OF VICE'S TRAIL - FOR WITH THE SPIRIT OF CIVIC VIRTUE STILL AT MY RIGHT ARM I WILL UPROOT, AND CAST INTO OBLIVION - THAT GERM OF SIN THAT SOURCE OF CRIME - THE "BRICK-YARD" - NO LONGER WILL OUR PURE POLITY BE A PREY TO THIS POLLUTION -

OH, PEOPLE - OH-H - POPULACE - YOUR "MAYOR" ASKS YOU - IS THERE - IS THERE ANY THING MORE YOU WANT ?

NO

HEY - PS-SST - 'S TEA TIME

YOUR "MAYOR" THANKS YOU - THANKS YOU - T-TH-H...

HERRIMAN

November 18th, 1928.

November 25th, 1928.

KRAZY KAT ❧ ❧ ❧ By George Herriman

December 2nd, 1928.

December 9th, 1928.

KRAZY KAT

December 16th, 1928.

December 23rd, 1928.

KRAZY KAT by Herriman

December 30th, 1928.

The IGNATZ MOUSE  DEBAFFLER PAGES

for 1927-1928.

1/16/27: This treatise on the transmigration of appendixes in Coconino County is probably the most offbeat Kat page ever printed. One suspects the inspiration may have been a recent appendectomy in the Herriman ménage, possibly with the ows and oys depicted here. (And boy! what we find out about the backstage machinations at Joe Stork's natal emporium…)

2/6/27, 11/20/27, 12/4/27, 12/11/27, and **6/24/28:** If the absence of these dates has alarmed you, fret no further: The strips that appeared on these dates were reprints from (respectively) 7/6/24, 8/17/24, 8/10/24, 5/25/24, and 7/20/24 – all viewable in the original Eclipse/Turtle Press volume for 1924.

4/10/27: "Hard pan" is a nineteenth century western frontier term meaning sun-baked soil.

5/1/27: "When you was a tedspole…" These are kat- interpreted lyrics from a popular comic poem spoofing evolutionary theory much admired and quoted in the 1920s. You can find it on the web, if curious. It has no relevance to anything Herrimanesque.

6/6/27: This page was reprinted as the second color Kat Sunday page on 6/8/35. No other black and white Sundays were ever similarly treated.

9/25/27: See page 118.

11/27/27: Occasional off-format pages such as this appear in the syndicate-released Kat episodes throughout 1927 and 1928. Most of these pages (possibly all) were reprints from years before (see above and below); they may have represented missed deadlines or ill health (particularly the four-in-a-row sequence, of which this is the second). In any event, all seem to have gone out in contemporary proof releases. However, some otherwise untraceable ones, such as this one (and 8/12/28, see below), may represent Herriman pages drawn and set aside when the New York Journal format was perhaps too suddenly set up. (See the previous volume for the details of this curious business.) In the Journal microfilm for the dates concerned, the off-format episodes are shown to have been printed on single pages rather than the usual two. A mystery.

12/18/27: The U.S. was still imprisoned in the depths of prohibition, as this episode reflects.

12/25/27: The "elephant's legs" is a natural monument in Arizona, as are many of the formations depicted in the page for 9/16/28.

2/19/28: All the artists referred to in this discourse on art gallery gazing are kleverly disguised kartoonists. To move right along from the second panel, these are Rudy Dirks, creator of the Katzenjammer Kids; Gus Mager, who fathered Hawkshaw the Detective; Jimmy Swinnerton, founder of Little Jimmy and Canyon Kiddies; Tad Dorgan, greatest sports page cartoonist of the 'teens and '20s; and Dan Smith, who never drew a strip but was a renowned illustrator of the time. Buddies all of El Herriman.

5/27/28: This and the following page reflect the famous early Sunday Kat sequence reprinted with lavish accolades in Gilbert Seldes' Seven Lively Arts of 1924, a work pioneering in praises for the good kat. 5/27/28 is actually a reprint from 5/13/23, suggesting that Herriman re-ran it as a "klassic" moment and then was inspired to create a new continuation for it.

8/12/28: Another mystifying "new" off-format strip. Did Herriman just ignore his stricture for one week? Did he dig out an earlier strip that never ran, as suggested above? Or is this a reprint that your humble editors have not been able to trace?

10/28/28: A rerun from 4/25/26 (printed in the previous volume) and has thus not been reprinted here. Perhaps the syndicate decided that the aggravation of reprinting off-format strips (or remounting them) was not worth it and decided simply to go back to the more immediate past for these reprints.

12/30/28: The major world powers were sinking some of their battleships in an orgy of peacemaking at this time. The Scottie seen here and on some other pages was a prime Herriman pet — actually one of a brace of Scottie pups who lived almost as long as he did.

KRAZY KAT By Herriman

This atypically maladroit composition, which was sent to client papers for release on 12/4/27, is in fact a severely truncated and remounted version of a three-and-a-half-year-old strip (7/20/24, visible in miniature on the facing page). Perhaps the syndicate, having run two off-format strips, was responding to protests from client papers by stretching this one on its Procrustean bed? (The original is viewable full-scale in the original Eclipse/Turtle Island 1924 volume.) The following week, the syndicate ran another off-format older strip with no tampering, after which new strips in the "contemporary" format resumed.

Collection C. Ware.

IGNATZ MOUSE
Des. and Copyright by Geo. Herriman
CAMEO DOLL CO., New York, Sole Licensees and Mfrs.
GEO. BORGFELDT & CO., New York, Distributors

IGNATZ

Des. & Copyright by Geo. Herriman.

This rarely-seen toy (actual size), fashioned of wood, reinforced rope, and molded composition material, was manufactured – probably sometime in the 1920s – by the Cameo Doll Company, and distributed by George Borgfeldt and Company, also the distributors of the first wooden Mickey Mouse toys. This "Ignatz" echoes the structure of the Mickey doll, but also that of the extremely popular wood-jointed Schoenhut "Felix" doll, likewise emblazoned with the character's name on its chest; while Herriman's characters predated both Felix and Mickey in comic strips and in film, his work was not as widely popular nor as "aggressively" marketed. One wonders whether Herriman actively wanted to exercise his merchandising rights with this object or was simply introduced to the idea by an eager and opportunistic manufacturer. Either way, it's interesting to think that Herriman may have actually had a hand in designing the unlikely item, as the label on its foot explicitly states. Many thanks to antique dealer Mary Ann Brandon of Illinois for contacting this book designer with the happy news that she had one for sale. – *C. Ware.*